SAVE THE ANIMALS!

by Annalisa Suid
Illustrated by Marilynn G. Barr

For Sarah, Catherine, and Tanya

Publisher:Roberta Suid
Editor: Murray Suid
Design: Jeffrey Goldman
Production: Santa Monica Press
Educational Consultant: Catherine Dilts

Also by the author: *Holiday Crafts*

ORDER FROM
BANKS SCHOOL SUPPLY
731 Billings St.   Teacher's Pet
Aurora, CO   Colorado Springs
303-367-5737   719-576-4011
303-367-5740 • FAX • 719-576-1224
1-800-228-2538

Monday Morning is a trademark of
Monday Morning Books, Inc.

ISBN 1-87829-46-7

✿

Recycled Paper

Printed in the United States of America

9 8 7 6 5 4 3 2

CONTENTS

INTRODUCTION

You are a concerned human being. The fact that you're reading this book is proof. You (along with a growing group of concerned human beings) realize the need to protect the animals and the environment. You understand that ecology is not a passing fad!

The official designated "Earth Day" comes once a year, but we must take responsibility for our planet every single day. We know that the destruction of even one more species is one too many.

Many celebrities have become animal rights champions, appearing regularly in the media and urging the nation to join the fight. But you can be more effective than actors or singers who are far removed from the lives of children. You, the teacher, have a direct influence on a large group of people that is here, now, and real.

Educators can go far beyond TV "sound bites" by offering in-depth information to an eager, creative, and open-minded audience. You have the opportunity to instill in this new generation a desire to help and to care. You can encourage children to value and protect the entire family of animals—from the much-admired whale to the often-slighted snail.

Save the Animals! includes scores of integrated-learning activities that will help you enable children to:
- Understand the term "species";
- Become aware of the concept of extinction;
- Realize the interdependence of animals and humans; and
- Relate ecological issues to the entire curriculum, and to their lives outside the classroom.

HOW TO USE THIS BOOK

Save the Animals! is divided into five sections:

Literature Links uses fiction and nonfiction picture books to introduce information about endangered or extinct animals, such as elephants and dinosaurs. The section's crafts, projects, and language activities help children connect with animals separated from them by distance or time.

Animal Awareness focuses on the day-to-day natural world. With the help of student-made bird feeders and other constructions, youngsters observe birds and other animal groups in the local environment. These projects teach children that every animal deserves attention and compassion, not only those on endangered species lists.

Kid-Made Displays, such as bulletin boards, books, exhibits, mobiles, and other eye-catching creations enable children to share information about animals.

Show Time presents songs, puppets, and costume patterns for putting on an animal awareness production.

Reaching Out involves students in ecological citizenship projects, such as letter writing, and newsletter publishing.

The two bonus posters can be used to introduce this animal unit as well as for classroom decorations. Certain activities in this book refer to information provided on the posters.

The main goal of this book is to help you help your students make their community a more aware, and therefore, safer place for animals. The idea is to change the world, and what better place to start than close to home?

TEACHING THE BASICS

Your students need to grasp the concepts of "species" and "extinction" in order to understand the need to save the animals. The following background information may prove useful in maximizing the value of the activities that follow.

What Is a Species?

Earth is home to more than one million kinds of animals. Each is called a species. Human beings are one species. So are dogs, cats, and ostriches. Two animals may look very different—Dalmatians and Dobermans, for example—and yet belong to the same species. The key is whether or not a male and a female can produce offspring. Because a Dalmatian and a Doberman can have puppies together, they belong to the same species. A Doberman and a Persian cat cannot have babies together (we don't have any "puppins" or "kippies" running around). Therefore, they do not belong to the same species.

What Is Extinction?

Extinction is a natural process that occurs when an entire species dies, and no members are left to reproduce. Many scientists believe that as some species became extinct, new species developed. Today, however, one species a day is vanishing. This rate is accelerating toward one species an hour. Some scientists have speculated that all species will become extinct, some day including humans.

Dinosaurs are the most famous group of extinct species. They were followed by very different looking creatures, including birds and mammals. In the past 5,000 years, humans have become a powerful species that has driven many other species to extinction—some by hunting them until no members of their species remain, but more often, through the destruction of species' habitats through land development.

In recent years, we have learned that the loss of a species can adversely affect humans in many ways: economically, biologically, and spiritually. We are able to invent many wonders in our scientific laboratories. But no one has figured out how to recreate an animal once it has reached extinction.

WHAT WHALE? WHERE?

Story:

What Whale? Where? by Edith Thacher Hurd (Harper) follows the narrator and a pal on an ocean fishing trip where they catch a . . . WHALE! The hungry mammal devours the boys' lunch, and then—still ravenous—rudely consumes their anchor. Although the children are frightened by the whale's size and temper, they overcome their fear and befriend the creature by removing the painfully lodged anchor.

Environmental Connection:

The population of many whale species is shrinking because of hunters who sell whale meat, oil, and tusks for large sums of money. Whales are mammals, warm-blooded creatures who nurse their young with milk secreted by the females' mammary glands. As such, they are closer to humans than to fish.

Language Extension:

In *What Whale? Where?* the narrator describes the size of a whale's mouth by stating, "You could put a skyscraper standing up inside." This is an exaggeration, of course. A more realistic statement would be that a whale is almost as big as a jetliner. Ask your students to describe familiar objects in new ways through use of comparisons. Encourage multiple answers. For example:
How big is your desk?
- Six telephone books could fit inside.
- A small cat could sleep in it.
- It's half as tall as I am.
- A whale wouldn't be able to fit in it!

Teacher's Note:

Give your students an even better idea of the real size of a whale with the pattern on page 8. Your class will be able to create a life-sized outline of a whale on the playground or in the gymnasium. Further amaze students by placing a picnic table or refrigerator box in the center of the "people whale" to represent the actual size of a whale's heart!

ADDITIONAL WHALE BOOKS: *A Thousand Pails of Water* by Ronald Roy (Knopf), *Humphrey the Lost Whale* by Wendy Tokuda and Richard Hall (Heian), *Whales* by Gilda Berger (Doubleday), and *Whales* by Henry Pluckrose (Watts).

HOW BIG IS A WHALE?

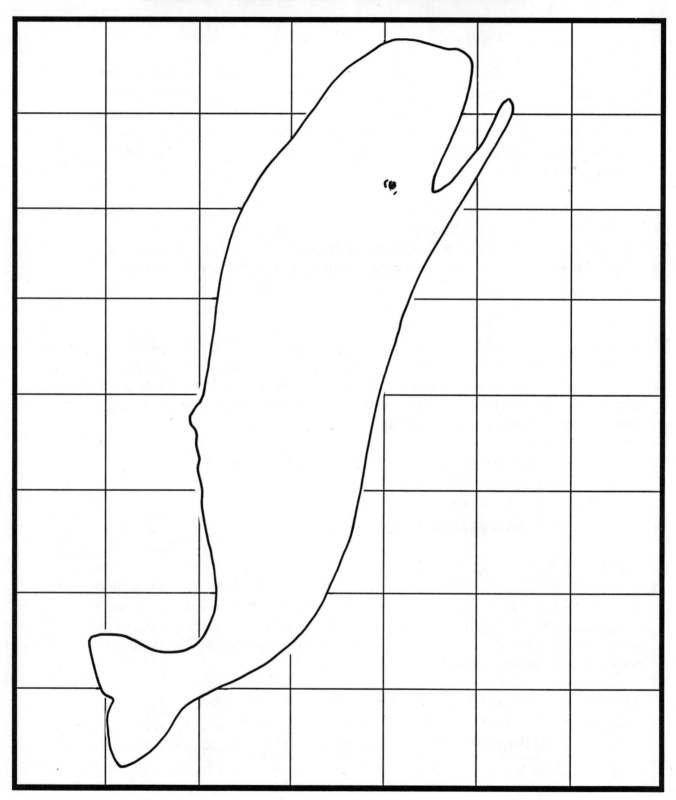

Scale: 1 inch = 7 feet

WHALE SONGS

Teacher's Note:
Whales "talk" to each other through noises that sound almost musical. In fact, people have recorded these whale "songs" to listen to for pleasure. (There are also recordings of other animals, such as exotic birds, dolphins, and wolves.) Different recordings are available to play for the children during this activity, including: "Voyaging with the Whales (an audio expedition to Alaska)" by Nature Recordings, and "Songs and Sounds of Orinus Orca the Killer Whale" recorded by Paul Spong (Total Records).

Materials:
Whale sounds recordings, tape recorder, blank tape.

Directions:
1. Play a few songs from one of the whale sounds recordings.
2. Have students try to imitate the whale sounds.
3. Discuss with children the fact that these noises are the whales communicating with each other. Have your students decide whether or not their own conversations are worthy of recording and listening to as music!
4. Dinosaurs became extinct long before the invention of the tape recorder. But that shouldn't prevent your students from imagining what those creatures sounded like. Set up a tape recorder, and have students make sounds that they think a dinosaur might have made. They can even pretend to be a specific dinosaur (a Brontosaurus bellowing).
5. Hold a concert of the taped dinosaur noises. How do these "songs" compare with those of the whales?

HAWK, I'M YOUR BROTHER

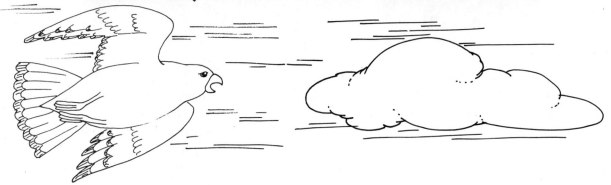

Story:

In Byrd Baylor's *Hawk, I'm Your Brother* (Scribner's), Rudy Soto has only one wish: to fly. He captures a baby hawk and keeps it on a leash for an entire summer, hoping to learn from his pet. At summer's end, Rudy is no closer to soaring through the sky, and poor Hawk is anxious to enter his rightful domain. Rudy realizes that Hawk needs to be free in order to be happy. Releasing his bird makes Rudy feel good, but enjoying a vicarious trip through Hawk's first magnificent flight above the Santos Mountains makes Rudy feel even better.

Environmental Connection:

Use this book to begin a class discussion about the need for wild animals to remain untamed. Humans have a responsibility to maintain natural places where animals can live. Many species in their own habitats—the jungle, forest, or desert—spend their time performing the same types of activities as humans. They find mates, build their houses (dens, nests, or burrows), and raise families.

Language Extension:

Encourage children to observe the types of birds that live in their own town. This will help them appreciate the beauty of all flying creatures while introducing the key science skill of classification. Have students try to identify birds in their neighborhood using the chart on page 21. If unusual birds are spotted, consult a basic bird-watching book such as *Birds of the World* by Lester L. Short (Bantam), *The Hayes Book of Birds* by Barbara A. McKean (Hayes Publishing), *American Birds* by Roland C. Clement (Grosset & Dunlap), or *The Bird Watcher's Bible* by George Laycock (Doubleday).

Have children imagine what it would be like to fly. Students can write about where they would like to go, what they think the world would look like from a bird's-eye view, and who they would like to watch them fly. Some children may want to write a poem, such as "I'm a Bird" or "The Day I Became a Bird." Others could write about their imaginary flying experience in the form of a newspaper article, or as an interview with a bird.

WINGS TO WEAR

Teacher's Note:
Paper wings can help children imagine what it might be like to be hawks soaring free, flying above the Santos Mountains and calling to their human friends below. Warning: Be sure to caution students that these wings will only help them pretend to fly.

Materials:
Heavy butcher paper, scissors, non-toxic markers, hole punch, yarn, glue, feathers, fabric scraps, crayons, "Hawk in Flight" poem (page 12).

Directions:
1. Have each student lie on a piece of butcher paper with arms spread out wide.
2. Trace wings (elongated oval) around the child's arms and shoulders.
3. Children cut out the winged shapes.
4. Have students punch a hole at each shoulder, and two holes at each wrist.
5. Children thread a length of yarn through the wrist holes to tie around each wrist, and one through the shoulder holes to tie loosely across the shoulders.
6. Students then decorate their wings with markers, feathers, fabric scraps, and crayons.
7. After the wings are finished, have children help each other dress as hawks.
8. Read aloud the action poem "Hawk in Flight" and invite students to act out the words as you read. Or, read the myth of Icarus and Daedalus and have students act it out.

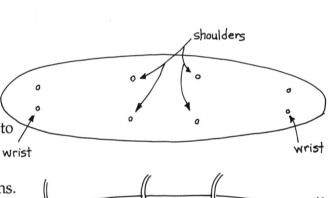

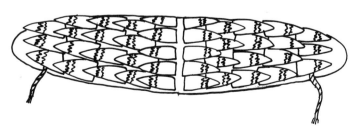

©1993 Monday Morning Books, Inc.

HAWK IN FLIGHT

Hawk, get ready to take flight.
Raise your wings up toward the sky.
Turn your head first left, then right,
Making sure you're clear to fly.

Up and up you start to soar.
Look down on the land below.
Circle two times, three, or four.
Now a light wind helps you go.

First you fly above the trees.
Next, the valleys, and the hill.
You float gently on the breeze,
The air moves you as it will.

Sleepy now, the flight is over.
Dip your wings down toward the ground.
Nature's runway filled with clover,
Now you land. you're safe and sound.

ELEPHANT AND FRIENDS

Story:

Elephant and Friends by Berniece Freschet (Scribner's) deals with one of the major causes of animal extinction—disappearing habitats. The animals in Elephant's neighborhood are dying from a lack of food and water. Luckily, Elephant remembers a beautiful forest filled with good things to eat. The animals trek to find the forest, but hunters attack the unfortunate group. The animals hatch a creative plan (along the lines of the Grimm tale "The Bremen Town Musicians"), and scare the hunters away.

Environmental Connection:

While this is a fantasy book (the animals talk to each other in English), the story contains many important ideas:
- A need to preserve wildlife habitats.
- Proof that cooperation can bring successful results.
- A message of peace on earth for all living things.

Elephant and Friends also dramatizes the killing of elephants for their ivory tusks. Because of the ivory trade, fewer and fewer mature elephants are found in Africa and Asia. Baby elephants, who are too young to have tusks, are tamed and sold to circuses, zoos, and theme parks. Much of the over-killing of animals could be avoided if people stopped buying items made from animal products.

Language Extension:

In this story, the animals cross a desert to reach their beautiful new home. Encourage students to write about a time when they moved to a new house or visited a favorite place. Or have children invent an imaginary location that they would like to visit. Have students illustrate their stories and bind the finished projects in a classroom travel book.

ADDITIONAL ELEPHANT BOOKS: *I Can Squash Elephants!* by Malcolm Carrick (Viking), *Elephants Never Jump* by Violet Easton (Little), *The Biggest Nose* by Kathy Caple (Houghton), *The Elephant in Duck's Garden* by Judy Delton (Albert Whitman), and *Uncle Elephant* by Arnold Lobel (Harper).

ELEPHANT BAG COSTUME

Teacher's Note:
Students put on these elephant costumes, and stomp around the "jungle" (classroom).

Materials:
One large brown paper grocery bag per child, scissors, non-toxic markers, construction paper (gray, cream, and pink), glue, crayons. Optional: peanuts.

Directions:
1. Have students pair up to locate where the eye holes go on their costumes. One child puts on a bag and the partner lightly marks the eye area with a crayon. If the bag doesn't fit over shoulders, students should make two side slits.
2. Children remove the bags, and cut out eye holes.
3. For ears, students cut out two large circles from gray construction paper, and two smaller pink circles.
4. Children glue the pink circles inside the gray ones.
5. Students accordion two long strips of gray construction paper (about the width of two fingers held together) to make the "springy trunk."
6. Children cut two triangles from cream-colored construction paper for the tusks.
7. Students glue the ears onto the back of the paper bag, the paper trunk at nose level, and the tusks at either side of the trunk.
8. If you wish, give each child a few peanuts to glue onto the front of the bag. (Make sure you have extras for snacking!)

Option:
After reading *Elephant and Friends*, students may want to create their own "beast" to scare away hunters. Provide them with paper, markers, and decorations to make creative, frightening beasts! Display their finished artwork on a "My Scariest Beast" bulletin board.

LET'S GO DINOSAUR TRACKING

Story:
The three children in Miriam Schlein's *Let's Go Dinosaur Tracking* (HarperCollins) take their grandfather on a dino-sized adventure. The foursome study various prints and try to guess what type of dinosaur made them. Certain tracks are very perplexing, which makes the journey quite informative. After a long day, the explorers return home, weary but filled with authentic dino-facts galore.

Environmental Connection:
Explain the process of extinction to your students. Although many animals today are being driven to extinction by humans, dinosaurs died off naturally. There are two popular hypotheses about the disappearance of dinosaurs. One suggests that these large creatures were unable to adapt to a change in climate. The other blames the crash of a gigantic meteor. Show students the map (page 17) that marks the locations where dinosaur bones have been found. Children may also be interested in knowing that humans and dinosaurs did not exist at the same time, no matter what the Flintstones say!

Language Extension:
Read aloud *Daniel's Dinosaurs* by Mary Carmine. In this story, young Daniel loves dinosaurs so much that he imagines them everywhere. The crossing guard is a dinosaur. Daniel's teacher is a dinosaur. EVERYONE is a dinosaur. (That is, until Daniel sees the sharks at the aquarium!) Have students imagine what types of dinosaurs their friends, relatives, and acquaintances might be. The drawings of dinosaurs (page 18) may stimulate ideas for stories. Bind the results in a classroom book, and have children provide their own artwork.

ADDITIONAL DINOSAUR BOOKS: *The Story of Dinosaurs* by David Eastman (Troll), *What Happened to Patrick's Dinosaurs* by Carol Carrick (Houghton), and *Danny and the Dinosaur* by Sid Hoff (Harper).

DINOSAUR FOOTPRINTS

Teacher's Note:
Students will enjoy going barefoot as they first become dinosaurs and make their own prints, and then become scientists to decipher their tracks. Choose a sunny day to do this activity outside.

Materials:
One long sheet of butcher paper per child, six shallow dishpans for paint, three dishpans of soapy water, blue and yellow tempera paint, towels, tape, tape measure.

Directions:
1. Make three dinosaur track stations by placing three sheets of butcher paper separately onto the ground and attaching the ends of each to the floor with tape. As soon as one child finishes making prints, reset the station with a fresh sheet of butcher paper for the next child.
2. Pour blue paint in three of the dishpans, and set one by each sheet of paper.
3. Place a dishpan with warm, soapy water at the opposite end of each paper.
4. Students remove their shoes and socks, step carefully into the dishpan of paint, and walk to the end of the paper, where they wash and dry their feet.
5. Place the yellow paint in each of the remaining dishpans, and have the students repeat step #4, walking at a faster pace.
6. Children measure the stride of their prints.
7. Students use their measurements to discover which prints show the longest and shortest strides.
8. Write the children's names on their experiments, changing each name into a type of dinosaur.

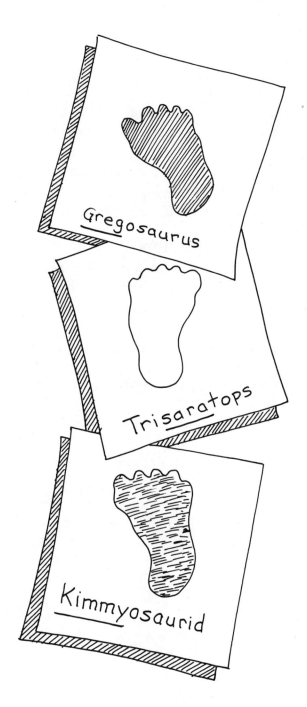

Gregosaurus

Trisaratops

Kimmyosaurid

©1993 *Monday Morning Books, Inc.*

DINOSAUR BONES MAP

= places where dinosaur
bones were found.

DINOSAUR PATTERNS

Allosaurus

Ankylosaurus

Brachiosaurus

Brontosaurus

Coelophysis

Dimetrodon

Elasmosaurus

Iguanodon

Pteranodon

Stegosaurus

Triceratops

Tyrannosaurus

TWO NUTTY BIRD FEEDERS

Teacher's Note:
Birds are always hungry, and are able to eat close to their own weight in food in one day. These feeders enable children to observe birds' necessary preoccupation with diet.

PEANUT BUTTER PINE CONE

Materials:
Peanut butter in small paper cups, tongue depressors, bird seed or sunflower seeds, string, low-branched trees, pine cones (one per child—collect them on a nature walk). Optional: if pine cones are not available, do this project using individual sections of an egg carton, a hole punch, and yarn.

Directions:
1. Children loop a length of string around the top of each pine cone. Or have them punch holes in the top of egg carton sections to thread yarn through.
2. Students use the tongue depressors to spread peanut butter all over the pine cones, making sure to fill up all of the little spaces.
3. Give children bird seed or sunflower seeds to sprinkle over the pine cones. (The seeds make the peanut butter easier for the birds to digest.)
4. Help students hang the cones from branches. Many birds like peanut butter and will enjoy this delicious treat.

The observation sheet (page 20) tells children what to look for when watching birds, and lists bird facts. Give students the sheet with drawings of familiar birds (page 21) to assist them in identifying common birds.

PEANUT ON A STRING

Materials:
Yarn or string, low-branched trees, unsalted peanuts in their shells. (Be sure to have enough peanuts to go around—there may be a few chickadees in the classroom!)

Directions:
1. Have children tie a length of string around each peanut.
2. Help students hang the strings from a branch; birds will find the nuts and enjoy a nutritious snack.

LOOKING AT BIRDS

You may see nests up in the trees. In the nests are baby birds. They do not have feathers yet. They are born blind and helpless. At birth, birds are called **newborns**.

Soon after birds come out of their shells, they grow soft, fuzzy down. They still cannot get food for themselves. Their parents take care of them. Birds at this stage are called **nestlings**.

Baby birds begin to grow. Soon they have wing and tail feathers. Now they are ready to leave the nest or "fledge," and are called **fledglings**.

The birds keep growing and getting bigger. **Adult** birds find mates and have a nest and family of their own.

Birds need a lot of energy to keep warm. They must eat plenty of food to keep their temperatures up. You shiver when you are cold. Birds do, too. Shivering helps the birds stay warm. If you see a bird with its feathers fluffed, it is trying to keep warm.

Do you know why birds sing? Male birds sing to get female birds to come to them. Male birds also sing to tell other male birds to stay away.

Sometimes birds fly in special patterns. They may also move in a way that looks like they are dancing. This is called "displaying." A male bird's display attracts females.

BIRDS TO LOOK FOR

Chimney swift: The chimney swift looks like a fat crayon with wings. These birds build nests in chimneys. They fly very fast while looking for insects to eat.

American robin: Robins are very common birds in North America. You may see a robin leaning its head to one side. Can you guess what it's doing? It's listening for worms! If you see a robin moving its tail up and down, that means it senses danger.

Starling: These birds are covered with small dots, like freckles. They build their nests in holes of telephone posts all year round.

Rock dove: You might call these birds "pigeons." They are very smart. A rock dove can remember 300 pictures and tell them apart.

House sparrow: The male house sparrow has a black throat. The female is light brown. They work together to weave a ball of grass and weeds for their nests. The nests have holes in the side for the eggs. Sparrows often build nests behind shutters or under eaves.

WINDOW WARNING

Teacher's Note:
Birds can't see glass, and occasionally fly into windows. They can hurt themselves. Protect the birds in your neighborhood by using the following pattern.

Materials:
Bird pattern (page 23), non-toxic markers, stick-on stars or other decorative material, glue, scissors, construction paper, tape.

Directions:
1. Give children the bird pattern to trace onto a piece of construction paper and cut out.
2. Students decorate the pattern with non-toxic markers, stars, and other eye-catching touches.
3. Tape the bird art to a classroom window to warn real birds that danger lies ahead. Children may want to mail the bird warnings to friends who might have dangerous windows. (Perhaps create a "Bird Safety Day" and pass the paper birds out to other classrooms to make the entire school a safer place for birds.)

WARNING BIRD PATTERN

LOVE A LITTLE THING

Teacher's Note:

Although many small species are endangered, they are often ignored in the effort to save larger, better known (and loved) animals. This project aims to remedy the situation by giving students direct contact with these tiny creatures.

Materials:

Small plastic magnifying glass (one per group of children), Little Critters observation sheet (page 25).

Directions:

1. Work with your students to brainstorm a list of familiar bugs and other small animals (worms, snails, moths). Have children share information they already know about small animals.

2. Arrange for students to observe mini-creatures in nature. The whole class can study a single species (like a snail), and then compare results. Or have small groups observe different animals and then compare them. For example, ants seem to move constantly while flies sometimes stay still. Children use the Little Critters sheet to organize data.

3. Kids can role-play the animals observed—illustrating how each creature moved and the sounds it made (if any).

INFORMATIONAL BUG BOOKS: *Bugs & Critters* by Brian Holley (Hayes Publishing), *Bug Poems* by Mary Ann Hoberman (Viking), *The Beetle Bush* by Beverly Keller (Coward), *Bugs* by Nancy Winslow Parker and Joan Richards Wright (Greenwillow), *Bugs—Big and Little* by Alice L. Hopf (Julian Messner), *The Snail's Spell* by Joanne Ryder (Puffin).

FACTS TO USE ON A BULLETIN BOARD OR HALLWAY HANG-UP

• Snails move by contracting a muscular "foot." In dry weather they seal themselves into their shells.
• Of all the animal species on earth, 40% are beetles!
• Earthworms range from 1 inch to 11 feet in length! They are important to agriculture because they mix the soil. An earthworm has ten hearts!
• Ants can lift up to 50 times their own weight!

Option:

Children may want to write about a "day in the life" of their animal to share with the rest of the class.

Name: _____ Date: _____

LITTLE CRITTERS

For each animal that you see, draw a picture in the box, and answer the following questions. Did it have wings? How many legs (if any) did it have? What color was it? Did you hear it make any sounds? If so, what type? How did it move? Other comments?

	Wings?	Number of Legs?	Colors?	Sounds?	Movement?	Other?
Fly:						
Ant:						
Ladybug:						
Worm:						
Butterfly:						
Caterpillar:						
Snail:						

WILDLIFE PRESERVE

Teacher's Note:

One tree can house over 40 kinds of animals! That's why it's so devastating—biologically speaking—when forests are cleared. Fortunately, certain animals are able to survive even after the wilderness has disappeared: birds, squirrels, mice, and thousands of insects adapt themselves to our yards, school grounds, and other urban settings. Encourage these critters with a mini-nature preserve built just for them.

Materials:

Small fenced-off area in playground (or large window box and dirt), seeds for grasses, berry bushes (snowberries and blueberries are animal favorites), small pieces of dead wood, shallow bowl or pan of water.

Directions:

1. Have children plant seeds for grasses (and other plants that are suited to your environment) in a window box or small plot of schoolyard. If there is room, plant a small berry bush. Birds and other animals will feed on it.

2. Students should scatter pieces of dead wood in a corner of the plot or put small twigs in the window box. Many insects live in dead wood and birds then feed on the insects. Warn children not to turn over the wood after it has been placed—they could disturb an entire environment.

3. Place a pan of drinking water in the preserve, but keep it shallow (two inches deep or less) so that birds and other small animals who may fall in will be able to get out easily. Have students keep the water fresh by changing it every few days.

4. Encourage your class to watch for visitors to your mini-nature preserve.

Option:

Keep track of the animal visitors by making a wildlife preserve guest book. Bind student-drawn pictures of the different creatures into a classroom book. Older children can do library research about the types of animals who visit the wildlife preserve.

ENDANGERED BIRDS MOBILE

Teacher's Note:
Many species of birds are endangered. Some are much prized by collectors. However, the biggest threat to most endangered birds is the loss of their habitats through the destruction of forests: tropical, subtropical, and temperate. You can help children become aware of the plight of these threatened birds by making spectacular, colorful mobiles.

Materials:
Endangered birds patterns (page 28), construction paper, glue, scissors, fabric scraps, crayons, markers, yarn, hole punch, wire hangers. Optional: wiggly eyes.

Directions:
1. Allow children to study the endangered birds patterns, and then trace or draw their own versions of the birds onto construction paper. They may wish to make their copies larger than the original.
2. Students cut out the birds and punch holes into the tops of their heads. (For the birds shown with wings extended, a hole should be punched in each wing.)
3. Children can decorate both sides of the birds with crayons, markers, and other materials then glue on wiggly eyes.
4. To make the mobile, a length of yarn should be threaded through the hole in each bird and fastened to the hanger.

Option:
Decorate a bulletin board with the bird patterns. Facts about the endangered birds can be found in *America's Endangered Birds* by Robert M. McClung (William Morrow). Show students pictures of exotic birds in *Birds of the World* by Polly Greenberg (Platt & Munk). List bird information from these sources on the bulletin board.

ENDANGERED BIRDS PATTERNS

Red-cockaded
Woodpecker

Swinhoe's Pheasant

Japanese Crane

Rufous-headed
Ground Roller

Bald Eagle

Corsican Nuthatch

Audouin's Gull

Short-tailed Albatross

Noisy Scrub-bird

RAINY DAY MURAL

Teacher's Note:
Worms may love a downpour, but your class may get restless. This activity is a sure cure for the rainy day blues!

Materials:
Chalkboard, colored chalk, masking tape, endangered animals poster, endangered animals books (used in the Literature Links section).

Directions:
1. Let children browse through books on endangered animals and also look at the endangered animals patterns on the poster.
2. Tape off sections of the chalkboard and assign a different habitat to each area (ocean, grassland, mountain, forest, etc.) by writing the word in the area or by taping on an appropriate picture.
3. Each child chooses an animal to draw from books or the poster and draws the animal in the appropriate habitat. (Help students who have trouble deciding where their animal belongs.)
4. When all areas have been filled in, remove the tape and have students color in the borders to complete the mural.

Option:
Longer-lasting murals can be made if your school allows children to paint on the campus walls. Plan the mural first by creating the chalkboard version described above. Once the mural is sketched out, transfer the ideas permanently with water-proof paint onto school walls.

PAT THE POLAR BEAR

Teacher's Note:
Polar bears are well-adapted to life on ice. Completely clad in white fur (except for the nose, eyes, and foot pads), they have a layer of fat beneath their skin that protects them from the cold. These snow white bears were once threatened by hunters, as well as by changes in their habitat caused by oil exploration and land development. Luckily, polar bears are now protected by the countries that border the Arctic. The idea for this activity is borrowed from the book *Pat the Bunny*, which invites readers to feel different textures (from a soft rabbit to a father's rough whiskers).

Materials:
Colored construction paper, cotton balls, glue, scissors, clear cellophane, black non-toxic markers, white and silver crayons. Optional: wiggly eyes.

Directions:
1. Have students glue a cellophane sheet onto construction paper to represent icy water.
2. Children add a bear to the page by gluing on cotton balls to make the head and body.
3. Using black non-toxic markers, they draw a dot on the face for the nose, and two circles for eyes. (Or give them wiggly eyes to glue to the cotton balls.)
4. Falling snowflakes can be drawn with white or silver crayons.
5. Post the students' polar bear pictures in the library along with books featuring information about polar bears: *Polar Bear Brothers* by Ylla (Harper); *Polar Bear Leaps* by Derek Hall (Sierra Club); *Snowy and Woody* by Roger Antoine Duvoisin (Knopf); and *How to Hide a Polar Bear* by Ruth Heller (Grosset).

Option:
Make a "Pat the Polar Bear" class book with the children's pictures. Have children use wisps of cotton to make their bears (so that the book will close easily).

WATERCOLOR CORAL

Teacher's Note:

Coral is actually an animal—little polyps (backless sea creatures) that build skeletons around themselves for protection. Coral reefs are made of millions and millions of these coral cups joined together. The reefs grow when the polyps die and new coral polyps build their cups on those of the dead ones. Coral comes in many shapes and colors. Red coral, found in the Mediterranean, is much sought after for use in expensive jewelry, a fact that has contributed to its endangered status. *The Underwater World of The Coral Reef* by Ann McGovern (Four Winds Press), and *A Walk on the Great Barrier Reef* by Caroline Arnold (Carolrhoda Books), are two informative color photography books about coral.

Materials:

White construction paper, red watercolor, straws, scissors.

Directions:

1. Have students dot a small amount of red watercolor onto a piece of white construction paper.

2. Children blow air through straws at the watercolor, rotating the page as they blow to move the paint in different directions. More paint or water should be added as needed.

3. After the picture dries, students can cut out their coral reliefs.

4. Post the different coral configurations onto the bulletin board to form a coral colony.

Option:

Although red coral is the only endangered coral species, coral exists in many colors, including vivid yellows, hot pinks and magentas, sea greens, and all shades of purple. For a more interesting bulletin board display, provide a range of watercolors for the students to use.

EXTINCT ANIMALS PAPER QUILT

Teacher's Note:

In this paper quilt activity, rectangles of paper represent extinct species. The idea is to emphasize that each life form is delicate and unique. The activity can serve as a powerful finale to your endangered species unit.

Materials:

Colored construction paper, scissors, glue, tape or stapler, felt, fabric scraps, sequins, yarn, non-toxic markers, crayons, extinct animals patterns (page 33), and dinosaur patterns (page 18).

Directions:

1. Have each student select an extinct animal from one of the patterns or from encyclopedias and other reference books. More than one student can choose the same animal (although, unfortunately, there are more than enough extinct species to go around).

2. Each student draws his or her animal on a piece of construction paper. The students can decorate the pictures with representations of the animal's natural habitat and food choices, and also include reasons behind the animal's extinct status. (For example: a dinosaur quilt section might have glaciers and meteors drawn around the animal.)

3. Connect the finished rectangles by using tape or staples.

4. Display the Extinct Animals Quilt in the library for the entire school to see. Inviting local newspaper and TV reporters to cover the quilt story can extend the students' knowledge to the community.

EXTINCT ANIMALS PATTERNS

Passenger Pigeon

Dodo

Great Auk

Saber-toothed Tiger

Wooly Mammoth

Quagga

Ash Meadows
Springfish

Sea Cow

Carolina Parakeet

ENDANGERED ANIMALS ABC's

Teacher's Note:
Children will enjoy working together to make a classroom ABC book, or—for a long-term project—illustrating individual books.

Materials:
Construction paper, markers, crayons, decorations, endangered animals poster.

Directions:
1. After looking at the animals on the poster, or at pictures in books or magazines, have each child draw his or her own representation of an endangered species for the appropriate alphabet letter. Assign a letter to each child if the class will be making a group book. Let the children draw a picture for each letter of the alphabet to make individual books.

2. Bind the pages together to make one classroom alphabet book, or into individual books.

3. At publication time, invite younger classes in to listen to a presentation of the Endangered Animals ABC's. Have students read the book aloud while showing the pictures. (Individual children can show the pictures that they worked on.) Or donate the book to the school library.

Option:
Videotape the children presenting their ABC books. Show these tapes at Open House.

PROGRAM

Raccoon Rap
Panda Bear Patty-cake
Oh, My Darling, Mr. Gray Wolf
You're a Grand Spider
Grand Finale

RACCOON WOLF PANDA

RACCOON RAP

Teacher's Note:

Raccoons are a form of wildlife that children may be familiar with. If they aren't, read them the story *Clever Raccoon* by Jane Thayer (Morrow) to get them in the mood for this hip, funky rap! Although raccoons are not endangered, compassion should be taught for all animals, whether on a government list, or not.

Students wear masks (page 37) while reciting the "Raccoon Rap."

RACCOON RAP

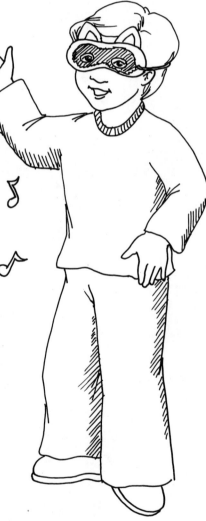

Hey, everyone, let's play a game!
I'll give you clues. You guess my name.

I'm a nocturnal creature—I'm up at night.
I sleep all day, but at night I fight.

I wear a mask—I make folks mad,
By stealing food. They call me bad.

My fur is gray. I've rings on my tail.
I'll eat right from your garbage pail!

I hold onto objects with paws like a hand.
I like things that glitter. I think they're grand.

On TV, Davy Crockett wore my hide as a cap.
Yeah, I'm a raccoon and this is my rap!

RACCOON MASK PATTERN

Materials:
Black felt, scissors, hole punch, yarn, chalk. (Note: you can substitute black construction paper for felt.)

Directions:
1. Have students trace the pattern (see below) onto black felt using a piece of chalk. (Errors made in chalk are easily erased.)
2. Children cut out the mask.
3. Help students mark where eye holes should be, and cut out.
4. Children punch one hole on each side of the mask, thread a separate length of yarn through each hole, and knot the ends of the yarn at the holes to secure. (The two pieces of yarn make the mask easier to adjust.)

PANDA BEAR PATTY-CAKE

Teacher's Note:

The Giant Panda is the symbol of the World Wildlife Fund. Although it is bear-like in appearance, anatomically it is more like the raccoon. Pandas are threatened by loss of habitat and destruction of their staple food—bamboo.

Put on a panda presentation with the following patty-cake rhyme performed in paper plate masks (page 39). Children can borrow the hand motions from the original "Baker's Man" rhyme, or march with their bamboo wands held like batons.

PANDA BEAR PATTY-CAKE
(To the tune of "Patty-cake, Patty-cake, Baker's Man.")

Panda Bear, Panda Bear,
Black and white.
Lives in China,
Is quite a sight.

Panda Bear, Panda Bear,
Eats bamboo.
This tall, tough grass
Is hard to chew.

Panda Bear, Panda Bear,
Growing rare.
Food's hard to find,
And it's not fair.

Panda Bear, Panda Bear,
Don't feel blue.
We're trying hard
To protect you.

PANDA MASK AND BAMBOO WAND

Materials:

Paper plates; scissors; black and pink non-toxic markers; black, yellow, green construction paper; hole punch; gummed hole reinforcers; yarn; glue; paper towel tubes. Optional: green leaves.

Directions:

Panda Mask:

1. Have students pair up. One student holds a plate up to his or her face while the partner gently marks where the eye holes belong.

2. Lower the plates and cut out eye holes.

3. Students color the panda masks with markers—black circles around the eyes, flat black nose, and mouth with pink tongue. Or they can cut features out of colored construction paper and glue them onto the plate.

4. Two half circles cut from black construction paper make the panda's ears. (They should be about the size of a child's palm.) Students glue the ears onto the mask.

5. Have children punch a hole on each side of the panda face at cheek level, and use gummed hole reinforcers to keep the masks from tearing.

6. Students tie a piece of yarn to each hole. (The yarn lengths hold the mask on when tied together behind the student's head.)

Bamboo Wand:

1. Children cut yellow and green construction paper into strips lengthwise, and glue the strips onto a towel tube.

2. Real leaves can be glued onto the top of the tube for a more festive wand.

OH, MY DARLING, MR. GRAY WOLF

Teacher's Note:
Gray wolves have gotten a bad reputation. While attacks on people by wolves are rare, stories of attacks are common. In the past, humans hunted the wolves mostly out of fear. Today, gray wolves are also hunted because they eat farm stock. Students make their own wolf ears (page 41) to wear while singing this song.

OH, MY DARLING, MR. GRAY WOLF
(To the tune of "Oh, My Darling, Clementine.")

Once the gray wolf was more common
Than all mammals but our kind,
Who lived in the temperate regions,
Now he's growing hard to find.

Oh, the gray wolf is a rare wolf.
His cry makes our pulse quicken,
But he seldom attacks people.
He prefers eating chicken.

Gray wolves fight against a bad rep
Given them by fairy tales.
Most people don't want to help them,
They would rather save the whales!

Due to habitat destruction,
Competition by humans,
We have killed off many gray wolves.
Now we must save all we can.

Mr. Gray Wolf, now we're trying,
For we want to see you free.
We should not cause your extinction.
We're responding to that plea.

WOLF EARS

Teacher's Note:
Children can sing "Oh, My Darling, Mr. Gray Wolf" while wearing the wolf ears. Complete this simple costume with whiskers drawn on with eyebrow pencil, and white socks worn on the hands for paws.

Materials:
Gray construction paper strips, sheets of pink and gray construction paper, glue, tape, scissors, non-toxic marker.

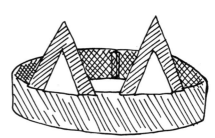

Directions:
1. Students tape two strips of gray construction paper end to end to form one long strip.
2. Have children wrap strip around head (like a headband) and mark where the strip fits snugly.
3. The excess paper should be cut off, and the ends of the strip taped together to form a headband.
4. Two triangles (about the size of tortilla chips) cut from the gray construction paper make the outer ears.
5. Two smaller triangles cut from the pink construction paper fit inside the gray triangles to form the inner ears.
6. Students glue the pink triangles into the gray triangles, and the ears onto the front of the headband.

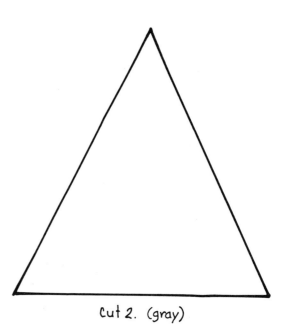

Cut 2. (gray)

2 strips end to end (gray)

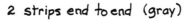
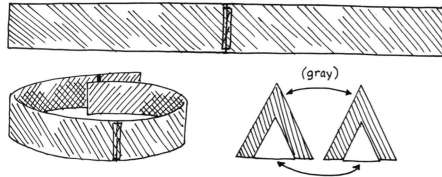

(gray)

(pink)

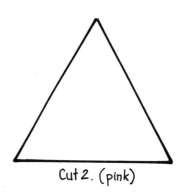

Cut 2. (pink)

YOU'RE A GRAND SPIDER

Teacher's Note:

Many types of spiders are endangered, from the Red-kneed Tarantula found in deserts to the Glacier Bay Wolf Spider found only in polar regions. Children who are frightened by spiders may warm up to these critters after reading or listening to *Charlotte's Web* by E.B. White. The following silly song may make them smile when they think of spiders. In a presentation of "You're a Grand Spider," students bob their Spider Puppets (page 43) in time with the music.

YOU'RE A GRAND SPIDER
(To the tune of "You're a Grand Ol' Flag.")

Do you have eight legs?
Did you hatch from an egg?
Do you hang from a thread in my room?
Is a juicy fly,
A meal you'd try
To lure in your web and consume?

You use fine silk thread
To build a trap insects dread,
And to catch all your victims and prey.
For, when it comes to gobbling pests,
You beat bug zappers any day!

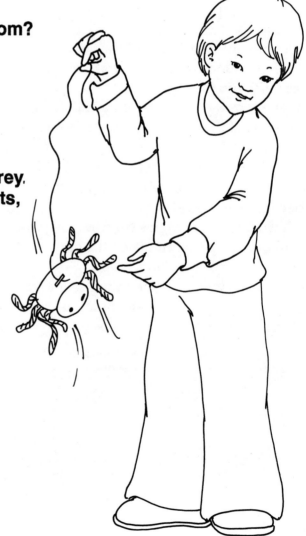

SPIDER PUPPET

Materials:
Elastic string (one arm's length per child), black and red construction paper, scissors, black yarn, stapler, glue.

Directions:
1. For the spider's head and body, students can cut two circles from the black construction paper. One piece should be the size of a baseball, the other about half that size.
2. Children glue the smaller circle onto the larger one, overlapping the two slightly.
3. Two eyes can be cut from the red construction paper and glued to the spider's head, or features can be drawn onto the spider's face.
4. Have students cut eight leg-sized lengths of black yarn and glue four to each side of the spider's body.
5. The elastic string should be glued or stapled to the back of the spider.
6. When the spider is dry, students make it bounce and jump by pulling on the string.

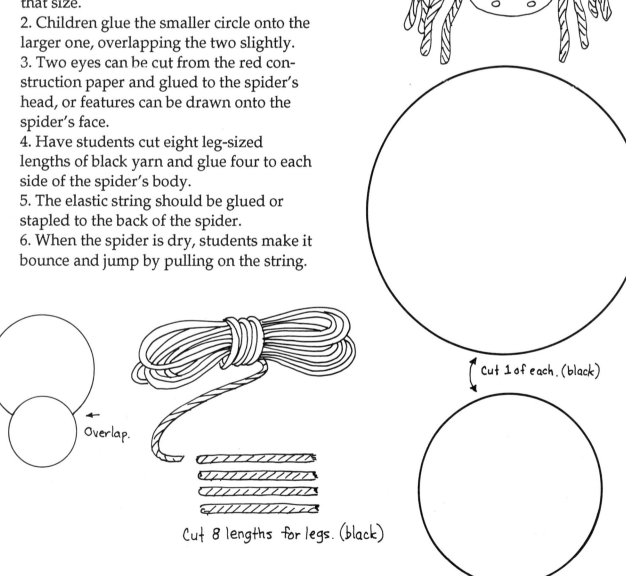

Overlap.

Cut 8 lengths for legs. (black)

Cut 1 of each. (black)

GRAND FINALE

Teacher's Note:
At the end of your show, let the students come out in their different animal costumes—raccoon, panda bear, gray wolf, and spider puppets—to sing a grand finale.

OH, GIVE ME A BREAK
(To the tune of "Home on the Range.")

Oh, give me a break,
Hissed the old rattlesnake,
As it slithered and looked for a home.
I'm from Mexico,
But have no place to go,
Since folks build towns where I like to roam.

Yes, yes, I agree,
Said the West African manatee.
I'm hunted all day,
If I enter a bay.
Pretty soon there will be none of me.

Please don't look at us,
Said a rhinoceros
Who was standing near a Great Bustard.
I'm killed for my horns,
And poached evenings and morns.
We live lives that are growing quite hard.

Home, home on the range.
Fewer animals have space to play.
What needs to be heard,
Are encouraging words.
Once they're gone, we'll have nothing to say.

ANIMAL AWARENESS NEWSLETTER

Materials:
Newsletter pattern (page 46), newspaper and magazine articles, and endangered animals books and materials.

Directions:
Students can work on this as a class project. With a monthly awareness newsletter, they can share information with the rest of the school, their parents, and other members of the community. As the ancient statesman Seneca said, "While we teach, we learn."

An interesting newsletter could include information about your chosen endangered animal of the month. It might also feature a column about the projects that children are currently working on. Pictures of animals can be drawn by students based on illustrations found in books.

Provide information about household pets and neighborhood animals. We have a responsibility to care for all animals, not just those on an endangered species list. This section could list information from the SPCA about spaying and neutering. One month you may want to include ways to handle an injured animal. You can get this type of information from a local wildlife resource center or from the library. Make sure to list people who are giving away puppies and kittens. This will help owners find good homes for these little creatures.

A lost and found section can help pets find their owners!

Information on animals for your newsletter should be kept in a file. Collect articles and flyers during the month, and sort everything as a class when it comes time to publish. Students should vote on what they consider important enough to appear in their newsletter.

Invite guest columnists to write for your newsletter. These might include your school librarian, a representative from the local animal shelter, a museum curator, and a local zoo keeper.

EYE ON OUR SPECIES

LOCAL NEWS

F.Y.I.
FOR YOUR INFORMATION

Watch for. . .

ADDRESSES

Teacher's Note:

Have students write letters to animal rights groups for information to use in their various projects. Or establish pen pal relationships with schools in different cities, states, or countries! Have students write on the back of the letter form (page 48), then fold, seal with tape, address, stamp, and mail.

Wildlife Rescue, Inc.
4000 Middlefield Road
Building V
Palo Alto, CA 94303

Animal Welfare Institute
P.O. Box 3650
Washington, DC 20007

Humane Society of the United States
2100 L Street NW
Washington, DC 20037

PETA
P.O. Box 42516
Washington, DC 20015

Greenpeace, U.S.A.
1436 U Street NW
Washington, DC 20009

Massachusetts Audubon Society
Lincoln, MA 01773

National Audubon Society
950 Third Avenue
New York, NY 10022

The Nature Conservancy
1815 North Lynn Street
Arlington, VA 22209

Timber Wolf Alliance
Sigurd Olson Environmental Institute
Northland College
Ashland, WI 54806

National Wildlife Federation
8925 Leesburg Pike
Vienna, VA 22184

Save the Manatee Club
500 N. Maitland Avenue, Suite 200
Maitland, FL 32751

Whale Adoption Project
634 N. Falmouth Highway., Box 388
N. Falmouth, MA 02556

LETTER FORM

Apply glue to flap, fold, and secure with tape or glue.
FOLD.

From:

_____

_____

_____

Place
Stamp
Here

To:

_____

_____

_____

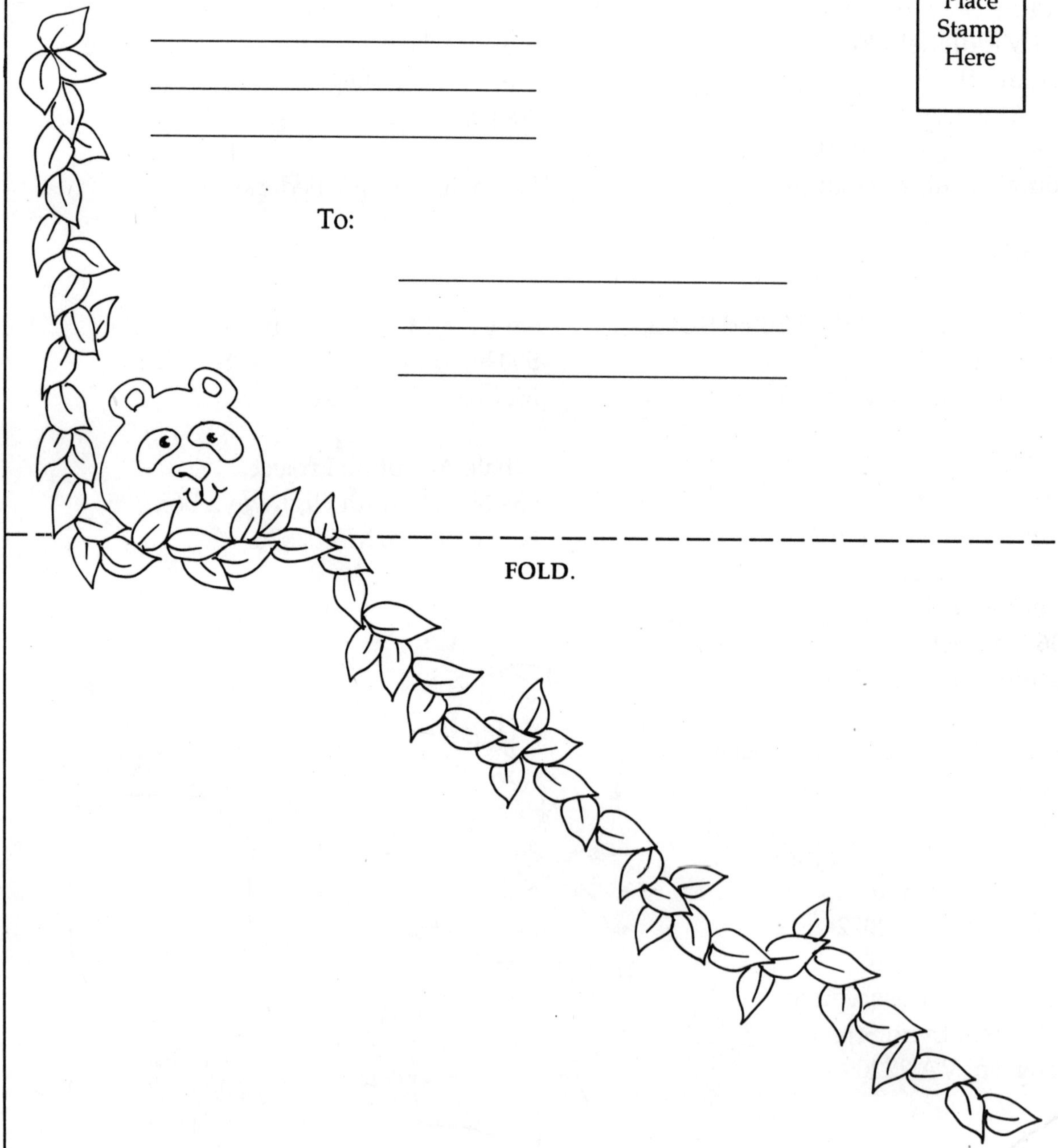

FOLD.